Frag... of the Mind

Jan Coulter

Dedicated to Linda H.Y. Hegland

Writer, photographer, mentor, friend

Acknowledgements

'Morning' appeared in the Taj Mahal Review, Volume23, Number 2, December 2022

Contents

Of Moss and Mushroom

I'll always be in your life, a
memory, a thought, a
twinkle.

Hold close. Now let go.
With heavy load,
I travel,

to the woods for protection.
Into the forest of sanctuary,
where pine cones arrange

themselves in perfect order . . .
A circle of mystery, into which
I stand,

shedding earthly trappings for
breeze upon my shoulders.
Naked, without judgement,

I am held fast to this place.
This liminal place where I am
no longer lost but heard,

to speak the language of
moss and mushroom,
Lady Slipper and Wintergreen.

Still, after the rain.
Lone crow caws yet
silent, a strange hush.

Air dense, heavily laden with
moisture, pushes my lungs
deep and deeper still.

I inhale the lesson,

memorise its verse, and
dance my way home.

A Cloudy Day

You hide your bruises well.
No screaming intensity
of colour,
no;

You bleed inward.
Warped tendrils of
hot liquid grief
wrap around a shredded heart.

You bruise,
from the inside out,
oblivious to those who look,
only to the shadows.

Market day, work day,
a cloudy day.
You, with sunglasses
shielding only shame.

There is comfort knowing
few will notice
your solitude,
your fear.

There is solace in
escaping prying questions of
gossip hungry minds,
which never rest.

I want to speak to you,
to reach out, to
hold your hand, to
comfort your aching soul,

but I too am wearing sunglasses.

Fragments of the Mind

I see beauty from a place of pain.
How else could I recognise your gentle touch,
amid the turmoil of storm.
I see hunger in your eyes which thirst,

alone on the landscape of thousands;
the cacophony of silence.
Voice muffled, stretched, mute to
ears which catch the sorrow.

Breathe into the hope of expectation
in the dark pocket of experience.
The sleeve on which you wear your heart
unravels, as wind pulls the thread

that stitched your soul of promise,
together with strings of sinew,
played like a melody, wafting on ethers,
Forgotten, fragments of the mind.

Leaf

Frayed, battered, edges curl,
grip loosened, carried on
breath of kind embrace.

Softly, gently; released.
Lifting upward again to dance;
descending.

Your stem a rudder, earthward,
drawn to rest, beckoned to place,
traveller of the fall.

Solitary Witness

Face down, arched, bent; the

smallest leaf is passing. A

graceful bow, almost apologetic —

other leaves gather close in grief,

reaching forward,

to hold her hand.

The Quiet

Quiet prevails.

No bird song.

No cattle lowing.

Even the geese;

quiet.

All is quiet, yet;

I can hear the

snowflakes fall.

Empty

There is something sad about
swings, swinging,
empty, in a
playground, where no one sits,

pumping legs like the
beat of a heart, a
metered rhythm , involuntary.
Lost in motion, like a

song without a melody,
pulling sinew from my heart, the
loneliness of squeaking chains,
swaying over grass scars

where feet drag,
slowing down the repetitions.
Never idle,
only empty.

Gone into the Silence

Like the seasons,
without a mention,
gone, on to the next
group of elements,
pelting at sinew,
tearing up walls of safety.

Power given away,
control — a myth,
yet within;
resilience, stamina,
always returning and then . . .
an absense, a void.

Cigarette's tip glows red,
burning the snap out of cold.
A chill to the heart,
reticent to succumb to
icy winds of change;
winds of solitude.

Somewhere between the
base and treble clef of time,
memory is unleashed.
Wafting up from
recesses dark;
a melody.

Song of lament,
refrain of passions past,
buried within time,
that cannot be held.
Silence that envelopes
time; that cannot be held.

After Burn

Shame, feel it.
Power, give it up.
Self, lose.

Ideals, be true.
Fail, the
audience notices.

What is power, when
given away?
authority over . . .

Idea, abstract.
Thought, intense.
Action, inert.

Power, a coercive force, or is that
corrosive?
Edges bruised.

The flame,
quick to extinguish, with a
long, slow, after burn.

Silent

Whorl of wing, soft squeak of
morning dove, jockeying for position,
within cover of close knit spruce;
planted twenty eight years past.

An aura wraps wisps of cloud
around an almost full moon.
Stars peek through breaks in cover, while
glass like flakes grace my nose and tongue.

Snow settles gently on
back of black dog,
filters into hill and vale and
changes the browns of thawed mud to

pearlescent crystals, perfect in symmetry,
yet each an individual,
falling gently as a feather,
silent as a memory.

Home

Shadows stretch long in
lamp light of the quiet.
Bend around corners,
exaggerate objects in their softness.

Listen to the cacophony of silence.
Speak volumes,
speak in tongues,
shout through mind's clutter.

Free frozen thought and inertia,
bend like shadow, lean into self,
travel home in the twilight—
home.

Release

Extinguish lantern,
long lingering shadow,
ember waning,
until;
darkness.

Angular, hard as coal,
black like volcanic glass — obsidian.
Sharp as an edge,
cool crease of corner;
night.

Slow, tender,
life's current travels.
River of breath,
carries the ache of life away;
release.

After Grief

Gutted,
searing white hot,
knife of abandonment.

Broken centre,
shattered edges,
armature cracked —

Let in the light.

Winter Cyclone

A crescent moon
hangs boldly in a
5am blur of
passing cloud.

Dawn's strength, a
mystery; with shoulders
set, night is pushed into the
breath of morning, to

rest in the envelope with stars;
their dust woven into blankets, while
moon beams tie this package of repose
into bundles of sleep.

Heavy fog rises above tidal river,
winding through valley floor, between
precious forest and damning clearcut,
held between mountains, basalt rich.

Winter's cyclone advances, where
snow will stick to window screen;
glass cold as the grave,
view obliterated by

perfect crystals, each a mystery,
magic in order and design. The tempest will
roar; but now we wait; the calm,
before the storm.

Buttercup

Fields peppered yellow.
Buttercup season.
Timothy grass laughs
with day's breath.

Ceiling low,
carasses in humid strokes.
Clouds leak and release
moisture, enough

to soothe
earth's cracked surface;
soft greens of new maple,
blue greens of spruce.

It is the fields'
unyielding yellow,
where acres of
warm buttery blooms

colour the valley floor,
altering the lens
through which we look.
Pollen collects upon my shoes and jeans

as I walk immersed in a glow
of thought and emotion.
Warm, soothing, restful —
the buttercup,

Boundary

Learn the lesson.
Obscure, veiled, hidden.
Gaze into depths of limpid pool —
Vision obscured by brackish water and
lily pad.

Hold within shadow,
imagination,
knowledge;
hanging like stalactites from
caves of experience.

Challenge observation,
render solution,
shun the echo of doubt.
Resist the pull to
retreat within.

Patch of Blue

Rain cries across window glass,
weeps into parched cracked soil,
nurtures new plantings, manna from
sky so heavy and low, its ceiling
graces tops, of north and south mountain.

Dandelions tightly closed, shield themselves
against pelting onslaught, and wait for torrential rains
to calm. Maple's extremities unfold,
gesture of welcome, hides its skeletal armature,
open hands, cupped to collect morning's libation.

Suddenly, sky retracts to reveal patches of blue, as
turkey vulture, solitary in its being,
soars on stormy thermals.

The Ermine

Grandmother winter sighs her chilly breath,
weaves her fingers among conifer bows,
caresses mountain, boulder and scree.

She cloaks valley floor and holds in suspension,
speech of hoar frost,
sliding into fields of stubble, snapping under boot.

Bracing gusts land droplets on snowy whiskers.
Wearing season's camouflage;
the Ermine turns to white.

Wedding Song

On this wonder filled day of commitment,
may grace weave your hearts together,
where love's strength flows within,
the metronome beat of beauty.

May arms envelope care, honour and
respect. Held within a kiss, constant and
deep as the tide, ongoing, everlasting,
days of understanding. Together, united,

not as one, but two souls, complete in
reverence of one another.
A distant view have I. Let me not intrude but
send armloads of flowers, framing my heart of love
for you both.

Morning

Dawn pushes night to rest.
Pale orange light on horizon,
like water. Clouds long,
thin, distant forms,
islands perhaps. Inhabitants
beckon paddle and canoe,
skimming silently, into the away . . .

Subtle glow of day break asks
eyes to drink in and view, a
white sheen upon the land.
Frost rolls into every hollow,
hummocks sport winter's breath, while
clothes line drips the hoar of night air and
sun's exhale, fades the chilly lustre.

Oh, how I wish my eyes a camera,
my lids, the shutter.
Fleeting images breed such urgency.
Time evaporates night's gossamer veil.
Day's canvas, coated with the gesso of dawn,
waits for brush stroke of day, while in the distance,
moon sleeps.

Awareness

Comfortable
with years of habit,
etched
along pathways of repetition.
Rhythmic,
slow, even breath.
Time,
escapes our grasp.
Dream
with running paws and
voice;
yipping in hot pursuit . . .
For your departure,
I am not prepared.

Discovery

Frost falls heavily,
visits low declivities,
crisp under foot,
shattering like fractured glass.

Puddles rest,
filled from days upon days, of
sharp, wet, moisture;
thin veneer crusts the surface.

Translucent film under which
water moves air bubbles,
trapped like struggling amoeba,
trying to escape.

New breath lives
beneath this prison of ice,
carved into undulating crevices, moving;
silent as a secret.

To Laugh

I wanted our love to laugh, to
sing into the fire, to
taste one another's essence.

How long have I known your
courage, your sensitivities, your
reserve of care?

You blew wind into my sail, then
sucked it back out.
I was fully clothed.
Now I am naked.

Grief

Polished stone,
we have become.
Smooth as waters that stroke,
Harmless, tender, free
to find our way home.
Human frailty . . .
The old woman did not return.

November

Wind kissed leaves, tossed on
air currents, warm, alluring,
sensual in their dance.

A beckoning from earth, a
need. Desire to caress the
fragile statement of life departing.

Prolonged drought. Trees parched,
hold tight summer's dress, to
quench their appetite for moisture.

Brown, curled, dried; with
last breath, wave farewell, the
bond with Mother Earth.

Release vestiges of summer.
Join carcasses, skeletal,
on this fertile land.

Of Magic and Wonder

I want to talk about tree swallows,
because if I don't,
one of these years,
they may not return.

A constant in my spring,
greeting me with aerial display,
gurgling their liquid chortle,
beneath sun's brilliant watch.

Vying for position whilst
choosing an apartment;
wooden box of peeling bark,
grey, weathered, wind kissed.

Nests woven mostly of white feather,
down soft to cradle three to five
hungry, blind, naked youngsters.
Yellow beaks wide, voices urgent.

The relay begins!
Parents in rapid succession,
keeping up the demand,
countless trips— and then,

curious babies, jostle for position to
peer outward, to catch a glimpse of
worlds wide, holding such allure, that
fledging begins.

Suddenly, without note of warning,
family of five are airborne, parents
supporting youngsters under wing, while
air currents buoy.

In less than a blink,
they are gone, hopefully
to return, for yet another season,
of magic and wonder.

Dance

Bend in unison, candles of dance.
Light our way to freedom from
thought and rebuke.

Lost in the flicker of flame;
dance,
the choreography is perfect.

Saturday

Cathartic,
straight up and down,
the rains.

Similar to emotion,
raw and humbling;
saturate a soul.

Drink moisture,
nectar of gods.
Taste sweet the freedom.

Smell through droplets,
leaf decay, apples and
pungent wood smoke.

Sustenance from the heavens,
we drink, taste and smell;
nourish our essence.

Etch deep our passage.
Sift through fecund earth.
Rest in underground myth.

It is here where I play.
It is here where I love.
It is here where I am whole.

Shadow

Do stars go out at night?
I think not.
Stars go out in our hearts, when

overloaded and hurting,
without comfort,
from self.

When our shadows grow long at
days end, sun slides closer to
mountain's edge. We roll up

our image with care,
curl within gentle rest, and watch . . .
Stars have not gone out.

Fragile Soul

Death leaves an open wound,
with sharp edges it weeps.

Rend the cloth.
A lifetime connection.

Cavernous void, a
chasm deep.

Ascend . . .

Fill this empty hollow with
crimson memories.

Droplets fall and leak from
eyes tired and weary.

Rise up from despair.
Welcome the dawn.

Spirit arms of comfort,
hold your fragile soul.

Frederick

The fragility of life
punctuated by precious souls,
we hold close, perhaps
not close enough.

You thought I was weaving
with strips of leather;
I noticed your beautiful hands,
Thirty-two years ago —

And now I grieve.

Arrival

Dew from evening's cool,
thwarted against air so warm.
Twinkling stars; fallen
moist, among blades of grass.

Birthed a chestnut this morning!
Twins, not identical.
Cracked, prickly, rust/green orbs, split,
revealing beauty; spring's seed.

Smooth, glistening; comfortable
in my palm of many lines.
Gentle contrast, to my
calloused hand.

I breathe silk like texture,
roll between my fingers their calm,
colour, rich as my thoughts,
taste, of comfort sweet.

Listen . . . autumn has arrived.

Of Winds and Water

Content to just be, at 3 am.
Many would think; idle . . .the contrary.
Mind visited, over and over,
a polished stone.

Thoughts jagged as wave lashed rock.
Winds create, recede; carving
fissures and fjords,
deep, within the memory of our being.

Soft and tender when oceans rest,
leaving pools in sun baked granite.
Gentle waters fill these declivities
where thought and reason thrive.

In Reflection

Afternoon sweats her way into
sultry night, slides in under
moisture laden cloud,
to pause in dark confusion,
nuzzling at restlessness.

There is no breath
to bend the flame of candle.
Wisps of hair stick, heart swells,
mind struggles with what was,
the here and now; a dichotomy.

Write in the present of
matters past.
Bleed with the memory,
call out with discomfort,
remember what was forgotten.

Feel the searing recall of
abandonment and rejection.
Regard now as courage,
rigid as its strength of weave; a tapestry.
Journey into beckoning light.

Question

If I really wrote from the heart
my bones would cry out.
Muscles strung taut,
raw, revealing;
a sense of shame,
so deep, so ingrained . . .

To overcome—a lifetime.
Parents gone, tether broken,
but not. Like a chain,
the weakest link is snapping,
and vulnerability is uncovered,
fleeing.

Painful awareness dripping like
treacle over my heart. In sorrow,
hearts shed, tossing layers to
paupers, who catch sentiment in pockets.
Emotion caresses fingers,
which curl around grief.

If I really wrote from the heart,
I would bleed, with nothing to staunch the flow,
no tourniquet to stave off abandonment,
no iron shield against rejection.
Without, every sinew . . .
visable.

Summer

Sultry, seductive, steaming, the day.
Wrapped in the humidity of summer's
temptress, vixen, she wolf; woman.

Matriarch of all seasons,
tethering us indoors to speak
from every pore, the language of sweat.

Close, heavy, blanketed burden,
worn under ceiling fan, where
blades blur against their syncopated shadow.

Hair sticks to forehead, clothing to skin.
Air hangs pregnant with moisture,
night promises cooling breeze,

leaves turn inside out while torrid sky
hangs lazy with soaring raptors riding
thermals in this summer's haze.

Markings

Bobbin lace, tatting lace,
Queen Anne's lace, all
intricate patterns like

palms of hands, each crease with
purpose, a lifetime
of experience.

Changing direction, melding with
adjacent lines, sneaking around thumbs,
marking longevity;

Coming together,
drifting apart,
returning to oneness.

Mirror of life's events, of relationships vast,
emotion depicted in finger prints,
growth rings in trees.

We are so similar in our markings,
So diverse in activity but each
returning to centre, to balance.

Stasis in life and nature alike.
Both experiencing seasons, yielding,
patterns of lace, filigree of the mind.

Fear Unbridled

Inner fear
blocks progress,
holds back spontaneity.

Awareness signals a
burning memory,
posing as a cloak of shame.

Lessons learned.
Lessons forgotten.
Judgement placed.

Scream, a lament,
inside the carcass of
insecurity and grief.

Pain and darkness run
deep as fjords, while
knife sears through a memory.

Photograph

There's a photograph drawing one
to walk a steep hill,
path slippery, leaves wet,
turned leather like from Autumns past.

Dark, dank, moist earth
heavy with notes of rust,
rotting wood, splashed slippery
By those who thirst.

Hand pump of cast iron rests upon
its worn platform; bolts and screws
set solid over time,
threads, long ago stripped.

A pool exists below pump's spout,
replenished with each use;
woodland creatures drink,
an oasis, the overflow.

Under canopy of maple and oak,
air rarefied, thin and curious for
those unaccustomed to dew drops,
veiled in dappled light.

There is a photograph drawing one
to walk a steep hill,
path slippery, leaves wet,
turned leather like from Autumns past.

Balcom Road

Listen to colours of afternoon breeze.
Taste richness of different notes.
Smell sweet strokes upon ones palate.
Know sensation in this liminal place of
ancient apple tree.

Halfway between here and there,
I will take you by the hand,
lead you into silence; so that
you may touch its vastness and
drink nectar of blossoms redolent.

I am no sorcerer.
Open hearts find this sanctuary, where
summer's insistence draws one in to
cool, moist, intrigue that
will not let you leave.

Weathered

Fence post peels.
Naked, bold, immodest.
Stratum of life's learning shatter
down its length, to hide in waving weed.

Grey of weather, graveyard stone,
grey of sinew,
buckled shingle,
galvanised by elements harsh.

In sorrow, hearts shed,
toss layers to paupers who
catch sentiment in pockets, while emotion
caresses fingers, which curl around grief.

We the weathered, the worn, the weary,
splinter as does the post. We are revealed,
tethered together, with winter's rusted wire,
strung taut at spring's insistence.

Post peels, bark of souls,
to the quick, to the centre.
It strikes a chord.
Raw at our core.

Abacas

Starlings in a row,
line up like beads
on an abacas.

Gather all clans,
ready yourselves, mass
exodus, fall migration.

Youngsters jockey position,
receive instruction for
long journeys south.

Straight lines, precision,
attention to detail. Careful
arrangement of varied species. .

In a flash of fury, all
wings take flight,
abacas empty, calculation interrupted.

So, in nature, it is true.
Silhouette, image black,
shouts . . . bleak and temporary.

Parallel lines, notes play upon staff,
power dances between poles,
clothes snap on a line.

Abacas lives in thought, a
meticulous art, rhythm of our days,
unnoticed . . .

Boarding School

Beach glass, shards of glass, crystal glass,
broken window, knuckles bleed, a parking lot, phone booth.
Skin cut, blood oozes, razor sharp.
Locked in bathroom, bars on windows;
someone jumped . . .

Evening

I creak up the stairs,
which also creak,
my shoulder creaks,
grasping for the banister.
For the first time,
I am aware of my tide clock,
Ticking, ticking, ticking.

Storm

Dawn sifts gently through my screen,
peepers cease, song birds sing
their morning anthem.

If I catch a cloud,
running under its black laden belly,
squeezing with all my might and majesty, I will

nurture land with moisture, with grace, while
turtles' breath moves maple attire
revealing skeletal armature.

Fear wind; its insistence, its rage.
Leaves turn inside out,
thousands of tiny umbrellas, green.

Fog rolls over North Mountain,
I fold arms around her ethereal self,
taste her silver passion.

Swallow thunder,
smell lightning,
listen to the quiet . . . before the storm.

Spring's Enigma

Content; my awareness
inspired by writings of mentors.
Anxious to unlock that which is hidden
from view. Eager to reach in, to touch;
sensitive, tender, bruised.

Blues and greens colour sentiment which
dwell in the dark recesses of my mind.
Rusting frame bending to
music of reality,
presenting verse to taste sunlight.

Verdant and ferrous scents wafting on
breeze of spring's enigma.
Earth accepting day's warmth.
Further moisture shunned, so also
tears grieving pussy willow's end . . .

Memory

Solitude interrupted, forbids rest.
Strum my heart strings taut.
Cello of soul, hold within, a lament.

Sing so quietly, heard only by moon.
Melody recall, pressed between pages,
waxed leaves, errant rose petals.

Collect from a time sweet,
experience, which
departs memory, leaving a declivity.

Divot of life plucked away,
fill with art, music and
 compassion.

Solitude returns, gentle peace,
silence speaks, cello remembers,
we are not alone.

Question

Where did you go into this dark night?
Returning with sea, fingers stretching to grasp shore,
encouraged by tide.

Did you rest upon sandbars with seals?
Their wisdom transferred to those who stop
with open and curious intellect.

 Memories are filed in recesses of minds, while
sensitive, precious, reflections dwell deep
within heart's secrets.

Tell me of the force that took you to sea.
I did not, could not, join winds that caught your sails.
Return with water's swell, relish soft embrace.

Tide will reverse to claim your soul, pull at sensitivities,
insist you follow . . . and you will,
go into this dark night once more.

Season Fleeting

Spring,
by waning candle in
disappearing night.

Evening soon,
folds itself into dawn,
day urging peepers silent.

Into mud, safely
waiting the next cycle,
possibility of finding union.

There is a sadness in spring's
brevity of fairy green
poplars, as they wake.

Pussy willows soft, alluring,
must touch, must brush
Across my cheek.

These catkins,
backlit by setting sun
reveal filaments of pollen,

waiting for breeze, or
passerby to help disperse,
so delicate, seemingly so fragile.

Rushing brook, sprouts
watercress beneath its surface,
trout's sanctuary between reeds.

Hiding above mud and rock,
Mayflower boasts a fragrance,
 fleeting once picked.

Impermanence of Mother Earth,
closes window of wonder,
Opens shutters of spring so short.

Mirror

To know someone, a journey
into self from the inside out.
Qualities not necessarily applauded, but
true essence coming front and centre,
to be cherished, to be held.

Subtlety creeps in.
Disguising features without compassion,
the kind that vanity recognises,
and mirrors distort. The looking glass
sees all, but acknowledges gently.

Look to the crow's feet that laughed.
Follow lines born of sorrow and grief;
corner of eye that still twinkles,
mouth that breaks forth
into that incredible smile.

Relinquish judgement.
Cast away notions of the mind.
Open to the magic of knowing
the daunting learning of self;
honour, trust, respect.

River of life, rapids in its path,
flows with an acceptance of change
Will such adjustment be welcomed?
With open heart and willing soul,
I shall wrap my arms around you.

Once

Once,
I loved; no —
I adored,
with wild abandon,
impossible to understand.
It was intoxicating.

You helped yourself to
the dust of my soul, the
marrow of my bones;
wove the sinew of my heart
into blankets of care, tossed
aside, no longer needed.

Rejected until I wept
between the lines of
explanation, your
paragraph of anger and
heat of disagreement
chill in the loss of self.

I cannot compete with
words of ridicule,
edges sharp with scorn,
a permanent crease in the
fabric of awe and angst. I am
balance between strokes of winter's chill.

I am reason,
I am understanding,
I am patience within
 the face of mourning;
for I have loved you well . . .
Once.

If #1

If I could catch a star, with
ropes hung long,
I would tie two together and
weave strips of twinkle dust, to
fashion a seat upon which to sit; then
pump my legs, swing high and
higher still, until my feet
touched the moon.

If #2.

If I could catch a star, with
moonbeams as reins,
saddled with the down of cloud;
I would ride toward Mother Moon with
stirrups of star dust,
kiss each glowing ember of milky way and
slide upon its path, while I embrace the light of
new day dawning.

The Breath

Afraid to wake, from
sleep that never rests, on
frayed sleeve, where
memory clings to threads,
bare and raw.

Pencil holds emotion, if
heart would relinquish.
Restless thought paces
through reason;
reality escaped.

Neglected and forgotten,
this piece placed,
to quiet a soul.
You have waited these
precious long years to hear,

river and lake call
svelt canoe.
Light of solstice, lapping against gunwales,
morning fog lifts as
bow splits the dawn.

Release as an elixir.
There is no smoke,
there are no mirrors.
The secret to wake, is held
within the breath.